kindle fire 7 9th generation User guide

The Complete Beginners Practical user Guide With Tips and Tricks to help you Master 2019 Kindle Fire 7 Tablet

Kyle A. Brown

Contents

DISCLAIMER

The information contained in this book is accurate and could be directly applied to the Kindle Fire 7 device. However, if as of the time of reading this book, you find any of the information in this book inaccurate; it simply means that amazon may have improved on the functionality of the device. We all know that technology grows as we humans grow. So, there is every possibility that the information in this may not be very accurate as of the time of reading it. Be that as it may, we are committed to updating this information immediately we find out any change in the functionality of the device.

ISBN.13: 978-1-6977-179-52

Chapter One

Unboxing the fire 7

We are going to take a look at the new 9th generation fire 7 with Alexa. It comes with 16 and 32 gigabytes. The 16 gigabyte is 50$, while the 32 gigabyte is $70. It comes in four different colors such as twilight blue, sage plum, and black.

This new table can work with a 512 microSD card, doubling what the last generation model could support. It has a 1.3GHz quad-core CPU. This device advertises up to 7 hours of reading, browsing the web, watching a video, and listening to music. It has Alexa hands-free and 1 gigabyte of RAM. It has a 2-megapixel front and rear-facing the camera with 720p HD video recording. It also has dual-band Wi-Fi and a 90-day limited warranty.

When you open the fire 7 kindle table you will find a few things inside the box, there are.

1. Small user guide from Amazon.

2. You will also see a small quick start guide.

3. Micro USB charging cable.

4. The device charger.

5. The kindle fire 7 table.

The kindle fire 7 has a speaker on the left-hand side. On the top it has a power button, charging port, microphone, 3.5-millimeter headphone jack, and volume buttons.

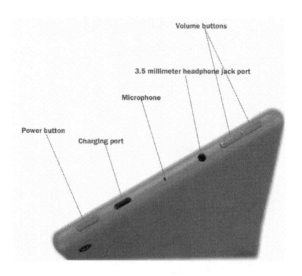

On the right-hand side is where your micro SD card goes. The screen is a fingerprint magnet.

Setting up your device.

When you turn on your device, you will see that as with all mobile devices, it comes with different languages allowing you to choose which language you want to use with your device.

Turn on your device, go ahead, and chose your language. And then connect to Wi-Fi. Your device might update for a while before it finally comes up, so you have to wait for it. You should click on the update to update your device when you are setting it up.

When you are prompted to put in your number or email for registration, you will need to click on the "New to Amazon" link. Follow the setup process. It is easy. Your device will guide you on how to go about setting it up from beginning to end.

Chapter Two

Getting started

This getting started chapter will help you do some essential thing in your device that will give you a delightful experience when using your device. I will be showing you how to declutter your home page, how to conserve battery usage, how to use the quick menu, and how to change the background image of your keyboard. Without any further ado, let us get started with how to declutter your home page.

Decluttering the home screen

When you get your device from Amazon, you will see pre-installed apps that Amazon puts on to your tablet automatically, and sadly you can't delete those; they are hard-wired into the tablet. But what you can do is put them into a folder, and it'll help declutter your home screen a little bit so that you don't have to look at all the apps that you don't use.

So, what you should do is to take one app, hold it and drag it over to the other app and then that should create a folder.

Once the folder is created as shown in the picture above, you can name the folder whatever name you like to give to your folder. Let's name that folder Amazon.

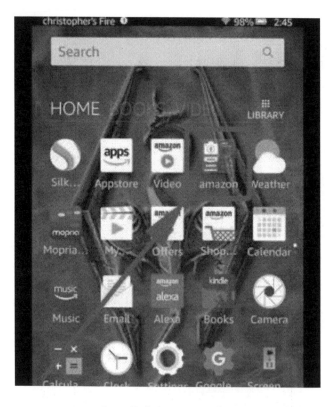

You can see the folder we have created in a red box and an arrow pointing at it. You can put as many apps as you want into the folder you have created, and you can also create as many folders as you want in case the one you have already created is not enough to contain all the apps. You can put all the apps on your home screen to only four folders.

What I do is to separate the apps I frequently use from the ones I don't use often. I put all the apps I regularly use in one folder and put the ones I don't use into another folder.

When you do this, you will see how arranged your apps icon on your home screen will look like.

How to reduce battery consumption.

When you buy your kindle fire 7, you may find out that the battery is not fully charged. So, you need to charge it before registering or setting it up for use. When you want to charge your device connect the USB cable to your tablet and your power adapter and then plug the adapter to a power source.

Sometimes, when you use another USB cable or power adaptor, your device charges faster. When you connect it to your computer, it also charges more quickly. But in many cases, the cable might not be compatible with your device, thereby leading to a reduced battery life span. I found out that each time I charge my phone with my computer, it charges fast but the battery does not last as long as it does when I use the electric power source. The battery icon at the top of the screen will display a lightning bolt to indicate that your device is charging properly. Next to the battery icon, you will also see an estimate of how much charge your fire tablet has left.

With low battery consumption, your kindle fire device can still maintain high performance as that is how it was optimized to function. Be that as it may, the life of your battery may vary based on the device settings. If you want to conserve the life of your battery, you can turn off some of the features and adjust some settings in your fire tablet. There are some features that you don't use all the time like your Wi-Fi. It will be helpful to set your device up to turn it off when you are not using it. This is how to turn off some features to conserve your battery life.

1. Swipe down from the top of the screen, tap Settings.

2. Tap "power"

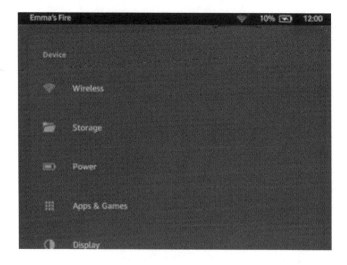

3. Turn on "smart suspend."

This will help you increase battery life by automatically turning off Wi-Fi when you are not using your kindle tablet.

You can also use the "scheduled smart suspend" to manually schedule smart suspend activities.

You can also adjust your screen brightness to conserve your battery life. If you want to do so, scroll down the page you are already on and select "Display settings," adjust your screen brightness and sleep settings. If your adaptive brightness is on, turn it off.

Move the slider to a lower setting in a sound notification. You can also reduce the volume of your kindle tablet to save the battery. Using headphones too reduces battery consumption.

Quick setting menu

In this section, I will be showing you what you can do with the quick settings menu functions. How to get to the quick setting is by your swiping down your kindle fire 7 from the top, when you do that you will see all the icons on the image below.

Let us talk about each of the icons briefly.

1. Setting the brightness of your screen. The way to quickly set the brightness of your screen is to drag the long horizontal line at the image left or right. When you drag it left, it reduces the brightness of your screen. When you drag it right, it increases the brightness of your screen. Sometime when you are in a dark environment, you may not want much light from your fire 7 to enter your eyes, so, you can reduce the brightness of the screen using that icon.

2. The Wi-Fi icon. This is where you quickly turn on and off your internet connection. In case you don't want to use the internet connection and it is already turned on, you can turn it off by clicking on that icon and turn it back on by also clicking on it. I have put the icon again in a square box below to help you identify it easily.

3. Airplane mode. You won't be picking calls while on a plane, so you have to click on that icon to switch it to airplane mode when you are in a plane. This mode takes you out of all your mobile networks which means your phone cannot receive any calls.

4. Blue shade. This feature helps you to adjust the color and brightness of your **screen**. It also helps to blocks blue light, which may make it easier to sleep after reading at night.

5. Do not disturb. If you don't want to be disturbed by calls and notification of your

device, you have to turn on this function. Just click on it to turn it on.

6. Bluetooth. I believe we all know the function of Bluetooth. You could connect your Bluetooth device to your fire 7 to play out the music through Bluetooth, or you could use Bluetooth for file transfer. There are better and faster ways of transferring files now that you could use, one of them is flash share.

7. Help. The help button will allow you to search for whatever you want to do with your device that you could not do. You will be taken directly to the customer support in Amazon to help you do whatever you want to do. You are free to use this service any time you feel like using it.

8. Auto-Rotate. You can either use the screen of your device horizontally, which is known as landscape or vertically, which is known as portraits. This icon helps you to alternate between landscape and portrait view. For the majority of people that like watching films, they can use the

landscape views to make the screen large. Sometimes, I also like using the landscape view when I am reading because I don't want to be scrolling left and right when reading some books. When you turn on this function, your screen rotates automatically to any view you want depending on how you hold your device. If you hold your device horizontally, it will maintain a landscape view. If you hold it vertically it will change to a portrait view.

9. Camera. You want to quickly take a picture and don't want to search for where your camera icon is? Then use the icon on the quick setting menu. Click on the icon, and the camera will open up, allowing you to take pictures.

Let us now go more into the main settings.

The setting menu.

When you buy your device, it comes with an automatic configuration, and you may not need to reset it anymore. Be that as it may, you might still want to change some settings on your device to suit what you want. This is the reason for this section. I will be showing you how to use settings.

There are two ways of entering into settings.

1. You get into setting through your home page.

2. You get into settings through swiping down your device and selecting settings

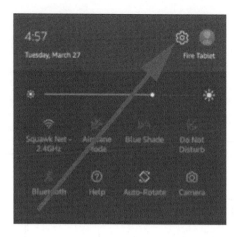

When you get into the settings, you will see many menus that you will need to work with to set up your device according to your taste. Now, let take a look at the menu one after the other.

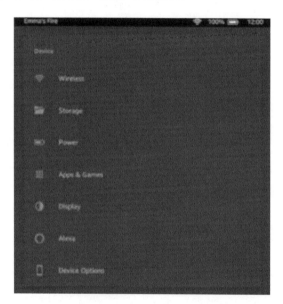

1. Wireless. This helps you to manage your Wi-Fi connections.

2. Storage. This is where you find your content and device storage options.

3. Power. This is where you can do your battery settings and usage

4. Apps and games. to manage your applications.

5. Display. This is where you can select your personal wallpaper and customize display settings.

6. Alexa. This is where you do all your Alexa settings. If you have linked your device to your Amazon account and the Alexa is still not responding, you can go here to turn it on.

7. Device options. Do you want to change your device name, access device information, change your backup and restore settings, and manage security features such as find your tablet? This is where you can do all that.

Under personal settings we have.

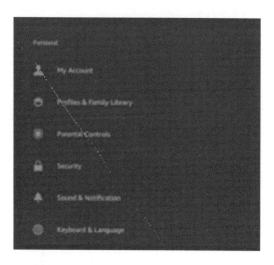

8. My account. This menu helps you to register your tablet, manage accounts, and connect to social networks.

9. Profiles and family library. You may have a large family, and you want to add them to your device for easy communication, this is where to manage and create family profiles.

10. Parental controls. If you bought the device for your children and you don't want them to access every information online, this is where to restrict them from purchasing content, web browsing, and access to other features.

11. Security. This is where you set a passcode for your lock screen and access additional privacy features.

12. Sound and notifications. Here you can manage your sounds and notifications. You can turn down the volume of the sound of your device. You can mute the notification etc.

13. Keyboard and language. This is where you manage your language and input methods. You can change your language in this area to whatever language you want to use.

Under the system menu, you will see the following.

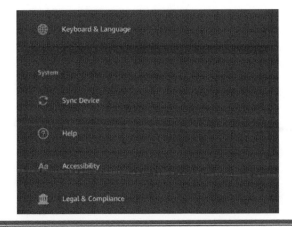

14. Sync Device. This is where you sync your device with your online content. This is to say. This helps you to connect your device to whatever you have online on the Amazon site.

15. Help. This helps you to assess help content managing

16. Accessibility.

17. Legal and compliance.

How to change the color of your keyboard.

I will be showing two ways you can change the color of your keyboard in this section. It's pretty straight forward, and I will be showing how to do so.

Method 1

Let start by looking at the default color of the keyboard.

You can see from the default color that the keyboard is black. So, let now change the color of the keyboard.

1. Swipe down from the top.

2. Go to your "settings." See the arrow below.

3. Go to keyboard and language.

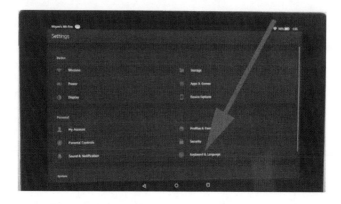

4. And then, find the "fire keyboard" option.

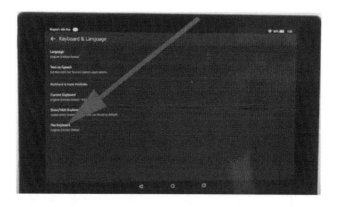

5. And then go to keyboard color

6. You have the option to change it to a "light".

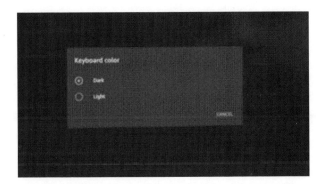

When you select "light" you will discover that the color of the keyboard changes.

7. Finally click on "light."

Now you have a white keyboard which is a little bit easier to see.

Method 2.

In this method, we will be using the Google keyboard, which has so many beautiful color and background embedded in it. You will need first to install the Google play store in your device before you can use the Google keyboard, so let me lead you to step by step how you can install Google play store in your device.

How to install Google play store in your device.

1. First go into "settings".

2. Scroll down and select "security and privacy."

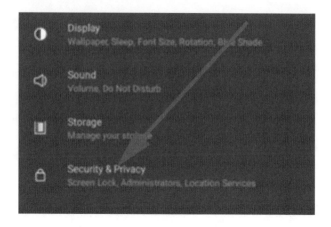

3. Make sure you turn on the option "Apps from an unknown source." This permits you to install whatever software you want to install.

4. Open your silk browser and go to google.com.

5. Search for "Add Google play store to fire table howtogeek" from the search result click on the link below.

6. Scroll down, and you will see four files that you have to do three things to. You have to download them, open and install them.

This is what you need to do to the three files, but I will show you what to do to only one of the links you should go ahead and do the same to the remaining three links.

I. Click on the link.

II. Click on the pink "Download Apk" button.

III. Confirm the download by clicking on "Download"

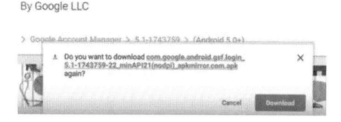

IV. Click on "open" to open the file.

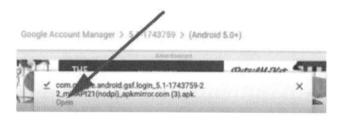

V. Click on "install" to install the App you just downloaded.

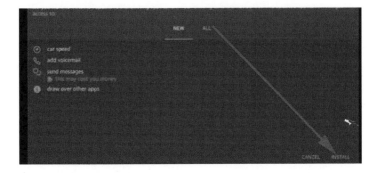

You have to do step I-V for all the four files, and then you will have the play store install in your device.

Changing the background image of your keyboard

We want to install the Google voice keyboard which will help us change the background image of our keyboard.

1. So, the first thing you have to do is download the Google app from the play store. That should be the first option in your search. Search for "google app." You will see the first app on your search click and install it. Look at the image below.

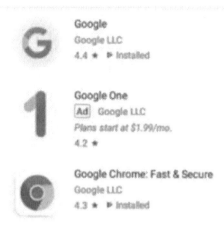

2. Search again for "Google keyboard" to download the Google keyboard.

3. Once you have done all that you will have the Google keyboard in your device,

which will look like the image you see below.

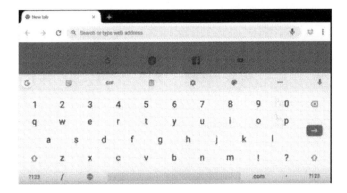

4. Click on the theme option on your keyboard, see the arrow below.

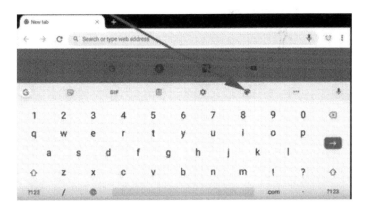

5. Google will bring out a lot of themes. You can choose any of the themes, and it will be applied to your keyboard. If you

chose one of the themes and apply it to your keyboard, this is how it will look like.

You can see the background image and the nice color the keyboard is carrying now.

If the keyboard was not set up automatically as your kindle fire keyboard, go to the app icon you just installed in your device and set it up. Click on the icon of the device, and it will lead you to step by step on how to set up google keyboard as your default keyboard. If you don't know how the icon looks like, look at the image below.

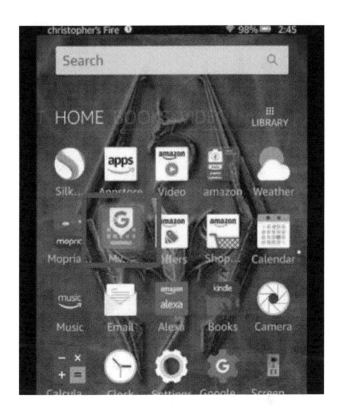

Chapter Three

Mastering the internet

Many of us are always connected to the internet because we may want to use social media, do research, read an online post, or watch YouTube videos. There are so many things you may want to do online, so learning how to use the internet with your kindle fire is very important. In this chapter, I will take the time to show you how to use the internet with your email, how to customize your silk browser, how to shop with your device and how to do proper research online.

How to Setup email, calendar and contact.

A lot of people use their mobile for checking and replying to their mails. So, when you set up your email in your kindle device, it helps you to check and respond to your emails quickly. I will be showing you how to set up an email in your kindle device. Use the email app to access and manage your email on your fire tablet.

You can add more than one email account offering combined or single inbox views.

After you finish setting up your account, emails will automatically be delivered to your kindle fire device. With many account types, your contacts and calendar will also be synced. Follow these steps to set up an email in your device.

1. Click on the email app.

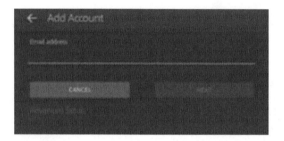

2. You will be required to add an email account, go ahead and add one.

3. Put in your email password.

4. If you want to create an additional account swipe from the left of the screen and tap "Add Account".

If the app you are trying to add doesn't recognize your email account, use the advanced setup screen.

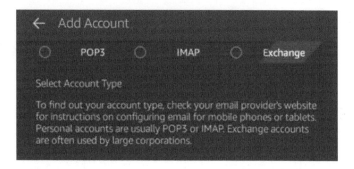

In the advanced setup screen, you can manually add your email service information. If you're having trouble or don't know your email account settings contact your email service provider or system administrator for more information.

5. To customize your email experience swipe from the left and click on "Settings."

6. Then tap "Email settings" or select an account. In email settings, you can change the text size of your message, choose whether or not to show embedded images, and manage other customization settings.

7. In account settings, click on "Email (default)," which will help you change your email account name, set a default email account, manage your sync, and data settings customize your signature and delete an account from the device.

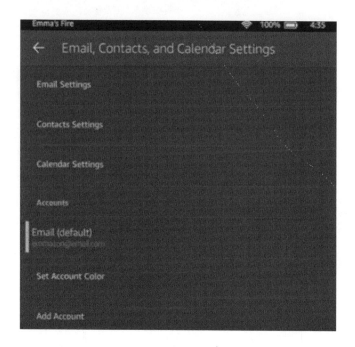

The calendar app.

The calendar app helps you to manage your events, meetings, and schedule. If you have multiple calendars synced to your fire tablet, you can select which ones you'd like to see. To choose the calendar, you would like to see first open the calendar and then swipe from the left and then tap the checkbox.

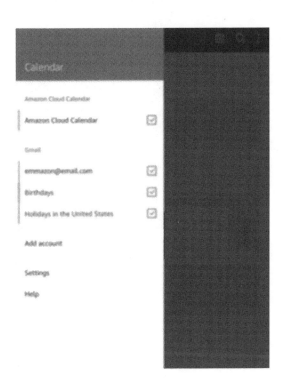

The contact app

The contacts app helps you to manage your address book and contacts. To open the contact app, click on the contact app.

Tap on a contact to access their profile page, and manage preferences.

In the top right-hand corner tap the star icon to designate a contact as a VIP, tap the pencil icon to edit the contact details, and tap the menu' icon to delete or share a contact.

How to customize your silk browser.

In this section, I will show you some quick tips on how to customize your silk experience Amazon's web browser. There are some options that you can play with on your Kindle Fire, and a lot of them you can access from settings. Once you open up "settings," go to "Applications," you go to "silk," and this is where the magic happens. Let go through some settings you can do when you are inside the silk browser.

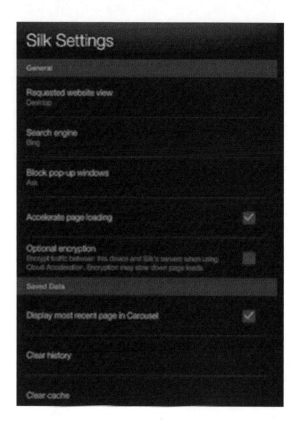

1. Force websites to show you its desktop view. You can decide to see the mobile view or set your browser to show you a desktop view. To do this, click on the first option, "Requested website view." You will be shown the dialogue box below to choose which view you would like to use.

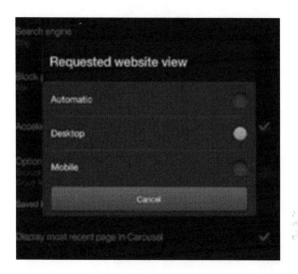

I chose the automatic view search engine.

2. Choose the search engine to use. You can select the search engine you would like to use by clicking on the "Search Engine."

The Amazon Silk browser uses Bing, but you can use Yahoo. Google is my favorite, but you can use Yahoo, Google, or Bing.

3. Block pop up window. You can block all pop-ups or ask when you want to get it blocked.

4. Encrypting your connection. If you want to pay attention to security and you want to encrypt your connection to silk, check the little box that the arrow is pointing at below.

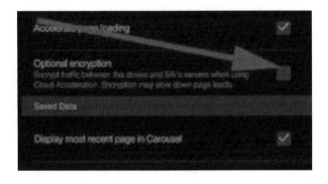

5. Clear browser history. You can clear your browser history by clicking on the clear history menu.

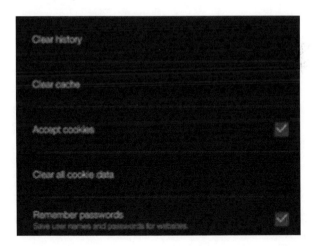

6. Clear cache. You can also clear your cache memory from clicking on the cache.

Cache memories are what the computer store up for you that you may never need. It slows your browser sometime when it becomes too much, so it is wise you clear them up once in a while.

7. Accept cookies. You can accept cookies or clear cookies any time you want to. You can also see the menu there.

8. Viewing data stored on each site. This is the cool part where you can see the different website settings and see how much data is stored for each website and delete them if you want. To do this, use the "Individual network data" menu.

This is very useful if you pay attention to details, and you don't want a specific website to have data sitting on your tablet.

9. Turn off your location. If you don't want anyone to look at your location uncheck the little box inform of "Enable location." I have it turned on; it doesn't matter to me.

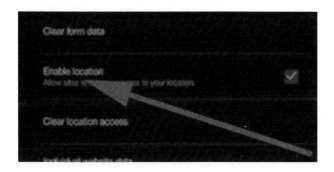

You can go ahead and play with the entire remaining menu I did not talk about and see what they have to offer.

If you play with this and you find yourself not being able to remember what you've been doing, you can just reset everything and get the default settings on your device.

How to shop on your fire tablet.

If you are an Amazon prime customer with a billing address and also has a one-click payment method set up in your account, you can do voice shopping with your Alexa device on Amazon. Whatever you want to buy, you can send the command to your fire 7, and it will process the order. Let look at a few examples.

You can say things like,

"Alexa, order paper towels" or "Alexa, add paper towels to my cart."

Alexa: "Alright, I've added paper towels to your cart."

"Alexa, order more dog food."

Alexa: "Based on your order history, I found a taste of the wild dry dog food with roasted bison and venison. It's $53.69 in total would you like to buy it?"

"Alexa, order trash liners."

Alexa: "I found glad tall trash bags, would you like to buy it?

"Alexa, what are your deals?"

Alexa: "I have several exclusive deals including Lindor chocolate, deluxe gift box, would you like to buy it?"

"Alexa, order Tide laundry detergent."

Alexa: "Tide high-efficiency laundry detergent 170 ounces, it's $32 total would you like to buy it?"

"Alexa order a hammock."

Alexa: "The top search result for a hammock is Best Choice Products Hand Quilted Fabric with Pillow Double Size Spreader Bar. Its $64 and 70 cents total. Should I order it?"

"Yes."

Alexa: "Okay, an order placed."

"Alexa, order toilet paper."

Alexa: "Amazon's choice for toilet paper is Angel Soft bath tissue, would you like to buy it?"

"Yes"

Alexa: "Okay, an order placed."

How to do proper research on the internet

This next one is going to be a really cool feature for the internet, and it's going to be a special search option, especially if you're using this for school, or research, and maybe you're on a site like Wikipedia, and you want to search out a specific word, this is how to do it with your silk browser.

1. Open the browser.

2. Click on the search menu at the top right.

3. It brings out that search box you can see there. Type in whatever word you want to search for in the search box, and click on search to search out the word. This is the same as using the ctrl+F on your keyboard to look for words in your Microsoft word.

Chapter Four

Working with Apps.

In this chapter, I will be showing you how to work with apps when using your kindle fire 7. You will learn how to install apps, use games, download apps, and forcefully close an unresponsive app. So, let's get started with knowing how to install the app on your kindle fire 7 devices.

How to uninstall an app

I will be showing you how to uninstall an app or remove an app on the new fire 7 tablets. Due to the difference in its interface, it doesn't interact the same way the older Kindles did, so the way you uninstall the app here is different. On the home screen, you're going to see every app that you have downloaded on the tablet.

If you want to uninstall any app from your fire 7 all you have to do is to hold down the app for a few seconds, and it will be marked.

Then at the top of your kindle fire, you will see uninstall. Click on it to unstill the app. As you can see, the good thing with this is that you can uninstall multiple apps at the same time. You do this by selecting all the apps you want to uninstall on your home page, and then you click on the "uninstall" icon at the top of your kindle fire.

How to install app

In chapter two of this book, I have shown you how to install Google play store on your kindle fire 7. If you have not read that yet, you can go ahead and read it now. After you have installed Google play store on your device, you can search out any app you want to install on your device and then install it. I have already shown you an example of how to do this in chapter two of this book.

Downloading app from Amazon

In this section, I am going to walk you through the process of how to download applications on your Amazon Fire tablet. It's a pretty straightforward process. On your home screen you're going to look for the little icon that says apps and once you find that icon go ahead and tap on it,

and that's going to open up the Amazon
App Store.

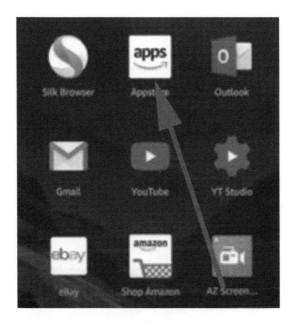

If you know exactly what you're looking
for, in the upper right-hand corner,
there's a little magnifying glass you can
click on, and then start typing in the
application that you want to download.

Let's say we're looking to download Spotify, so start typing in Spotify.

You can click on the first option that shows up in your search which is the Spotify app with a good rating, or you can use the orange magnifying glass on the right-hand side of the keyboard that has a little orange circle around, it will take you to the search results.

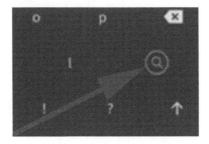

Click on that little tile and it will take you to the download page.

Over on the right-hand side of the screen, you'll see an orange button that says "Get," go ahead and tap on that, then click the green download button. That will go through the download and installation process of that particular application.

Assuming you don't know the name of the application that you're looking for or maybe you want to browse around and see what's available. On the left-hand side of the screen in the upper left corner next to home, you will see "categories" click on it. Then it will give you all these different categories that you can browse through.

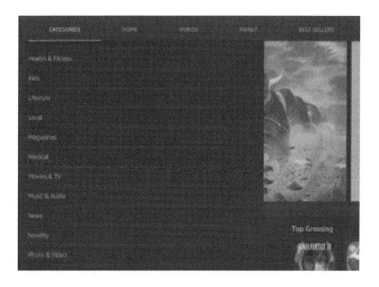

Assuming you want to look at what games are available, tap on the "games" option and then you can go down and search through all the different games categories. You can take the time to see all the recommended games, and then you can go ahead and scroll through and see all the different options. Let's take a look at candy crush. Over on the right-hand side of the screen, you will see the "Get" button if you want to download the application go ahead and click "get" and then click that green download button.

These are a couple of different ways that you can go about downloading applications on your kindle fire 7. As soon as you're done downloading and installing whichever app that you're interested in getting on your home screen, you're going to scroll down to the bottom of the page, and those icons will show up right at the end. If you're confused as to where those icons are showing up, that's where they will land after they complete installing.

How to close apps running on the background of your device.

In this section, I want to show you how to close running apps on your Kindle Fire. A lot of times you open apps, and then you go back to the home screen, but you don't realize that those apps are still running in the background and they can either run your battery down, or it can cause your Kindle to run slower because you might have too many things running. I will be showing you three simple ways you can close any apps running in the background of your device.

Method 1. using the "Advanced Task Killer" app.

Advance task killer can help you close any app that is not responding and also running at the background of your device. You can easily download this app through the Google store or Amazon store. If you have read the previous chapters of this book, you would have learned how to install apps through both mediums. Once the app is installed on your kindle fire 7 launch the app. Check the app you want to kill or close and then select "**kill selected app.**"

Method 2 using the features in your kindle fire.

1. When using this method, you have to press the **square icon** situated at the lower-right part of the screen of your device. When you do that you will see the open apps pops up as you see in the image below.

2. When you want to switch between the apps, you should swipe up and down.

3. Click on the "X" sign at the top right of the app to close the app. Or you swipe the app you want to close to the right as shown in the image above.

Method 3. Using the setting menu. You can also use the setting menu to close any apps that are unresponsive or running at the background of your device. Follow these steps to do that.

1. Open **"Setting"** in your device.

2. Select **"Apps and Games"** or **"Application"**

3. Then click on **"Manage All Applications"** or **"installed Applications."**

4. Swipe to move to the **"Running"** apps

5. Look for the apps you want to close, then select **"Stop."**

6. Then click on **"Ok."**

Chapter Five

Reading books With your fire 7

In this chapter, I will be showing you how to read books from your kindle fire device. When you have a good knowledge of how to use your kindle fire for reading books, you will prefer using your device for reading books instead of reading the traditional hard copy book.

One thing I love with reading books from a mobile device is that, you can read any book anywhere without anyone knowing you are reading a book. There are some groups of friends I will be with that I would not want to show them that I am reading a book at all. This is purely for personal reasons I won't like to give out my reasons here. For me, sometimes it is better to keep my study life private from some groups of friends. If you are like me, you may want to do the same, and the best medium to read books in the group of friend and it won't look as if you are a bookworm is to read it from your mobile device. And I am not saying it is bad to be seen as a bookworm, but for me I would rather keep that away from some of my friends.

Reading an Ebooks.

Different apps can help you read an ebook from your kindle device. Whenever you get an eBook, where purchased or downloaded for free, you should find out the appropriate application that can open the eBook. If you are reading eBooks from Amazon or downloaded from Amazon, you can use the kindle eBook application.

When you open an ebook using the Amazon application, you will find out that scrolling is relatively smooth. You can move from one page to the other by swiping right while the eBook is opened.

The reading experience is pretty decent. You get a fair amount of text on the page, and you can adjust the font sizes.

How to adjust font sizes.

You can adjust the font sizes by clicking on the page of the opened ebook. When you do that, it will bring out the functions that will help you adjust the font sizes and also do other settings. When you click a little bit hard on the opened ebook, you will see the following icons below the page you have opened.

To change the font size of your text simply click on the "Aa" icon, you will see the image below.

You can see that the "Aa" ranges from very small to huge ones. If you want your text to be huge, click on the last "Aa" icon to the right and if you want it tiny click on the first "Aa" icon to the left. When doing this, you have to bear in mind that the larger your font size, the fewer the text that will be contained in a page.

Adjusting the line spacing

You can adjust the line spacing of your text by clicking on any of the icon on the line spacing section of the image below.

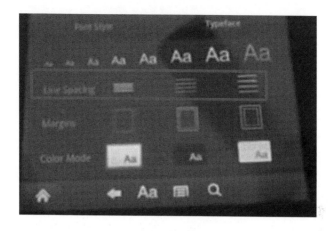

You can also adjust the margin of the text by using the next line below the line spacing. This is pretty simple and straight forward. All you have to do is to click on any of the three icons to adjust the line spacing.

Changing your page color mode.

You can also change your text color mode by using the "color Mode" section.

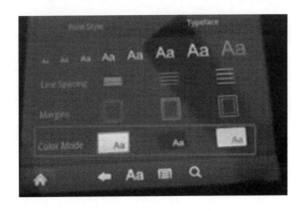

The first icon is the one that is always selected by default. You can change it to the one you one by clicking on any of the two icons to the right of the first one. You can see that there are not many options for changing the color of your text. But, I like the second icon because it is the night reading mode. When reading in the night and you don't want plenty of light to enter your eyes, you can use the night mode. This will make the background of your text black and the text white.

Changing your font type

Sometimes, you might get tired of reading the same font all the time and would like to change it. You can do so by clicking on the second link at the top of the image we have been using.

When you click on "Typeface," you will see a display of many different font types that you can use, click on any of the "Typeface" to activate the font type.

How to download free books.

I will be showing you a website for getting the books for the Kindle Fire 7 tablets. If you go to this website, you'll see they have tons of books they're all free. A lot of times you'll see a reasonably popular book or something that just came out. The publisher will put it out there to get a whole bunch of downloads fast for like two days or maybe for a week. So, you get some decent books, and there's a lot of crap books, a lot of short books that people wrote they want you to know.

There are many new upcoming authors with very nice books that many people have not known yet. Many of them would put out such books for free to get people to read their books and look out for more other books if they enjoyed the one they have read. Many seasoned authors use this medium as a way of reaching many more readers, thereby increasing his or her popularity. This allows you to read as many books as possible for free from Amazon.

The website is *freereadfeed.com*. Log in to the site, and you will see many free books that you can download for free. When you first log in, you will see all the popularly downloaded books on the home page. You can scan through to see if you would like to download any of these books into your kindle fire 7.

If you want non-fiction books, only, you can click on the non-fiction button on top of the page to download the non-fiction books.

Once you have found the book you would like to download, click on the link of the book, and it will take you to Amazon site for download. For example, click on the first book you see on the page below.

When you click on the first book, it will take you to the Amazon site you can see below.

This book is entirely free, as you can see. It does not have a paperback version of it at all. There are some you would click on that will have the paperback version like the second option.

To download any of the books into your kindle fire 7 clicks on the "Buy Now with 1 click" button. You will be required to log in to your Amazon account if you have not logged in yet.

When downloading from this website, you have to be careful because sometimes the free part may have expired, and the website may not have been updated, and they may be charging a price for it. So, be careful when you click any book because once in a while, they will try to charge you for the books. So, you should be careful because the free part may have expired.

This is how you can get as many books as possible for free to read in your kindle fire 7

Borrowing books from Amazon.

A prime member of the Amazon community can borrow one book each month from Amazon. There are thousands of titles in the library, including many bestsellers books that you can borrow from and read in your Kindle Fire 7 devices. If you have other mobile kindle devices connect to the internet, any book you borrowed can also be delivered to such a device if they are all connected to the same account. Book borrowed from kindle owners library has no due date.

From your fire tablet, open the Kindle Store from the home page of your device.

Tap all categories

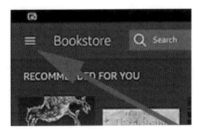

Tap "Kindle owner's lending library" and then search for a book you wish to borrow when you've made your book selection, tap read for free. You should be able to borrow only one book at a time. If you have already borrowed a book, you will be prompted by amazon to return that book before you can borrow another book. The titles available for borrow may change every month.

If you have borrowed book and you decide to cancel your Prime membership, your book will be automatically returned to kindle owners' library. Your notes, highlights, and bookmarks within the book your borrowed will be saved to your Amazon account and are available if you purchase or borrow the book later.

If you have finished reading the book and you want to return the book, go to Manage your content to amazon.com/mycd. Next to the book you want to return, click the "Actions" menu, and then click return book.

Chapter Six

How to enjoy music on your device.

In this chapter, we are going to be looking at Alexa music services and how you play different kinds of music on the echo dot or echo unit. We're going to take a look at Pandora, Spotify, TuneIn, and Amazon music.

We're going to take a look at the Alexa app because the Alexa app is what controls music on Alexa. In the Alexa app, we can sign into online music services like Pandora, Spotify, and others, and then you can control music on the Echo dot or the echo show using the Alexa app, we can also control it using our voice. Let's now go to the apps and see how this is done.

1. First, lunch the app.

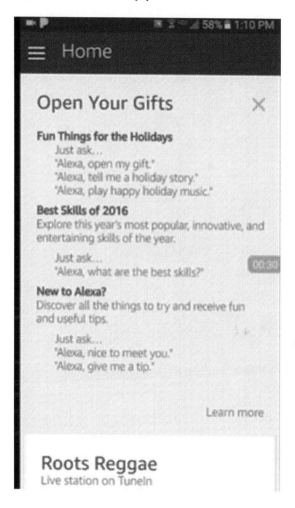

2. Click on the menu button, the three horizontal lines at the top left of the screen

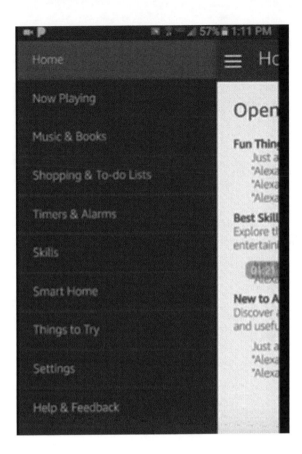

3. Select "music and Book" the second menu when you are counting from the top. It will bring you to the music area and then will give you the option of the echo device you want to select.

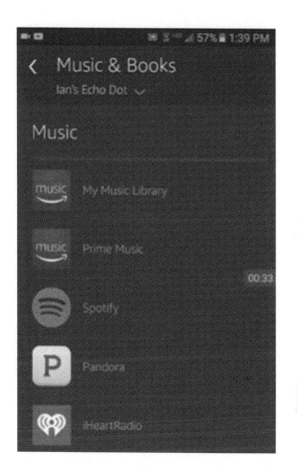

You can see that it has brought you to all the music online that you can select and start using.

4. Select anyone you have an account with. Let's use Spotify, for example.

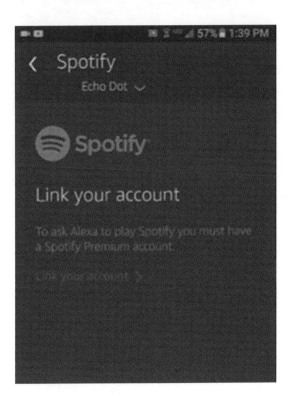

5. You have to link your Alexa device to Spotify of any other music channels you see on the app.

6. Once your account is connected, you will see all the available music, and you can pick the one you want and start playing.

The iheartRadio

You should follow the steps outlined above to get into this radio station. There are a lot of stations here that you can listen to at any time.

How to connect TuneIn

The ways you connect this are mostly the same. TuneIn is a free station, but it is focused on radio content, and it plays only music. For example, a roots reggae station that plays old reggae.

So, click on TuneIn.

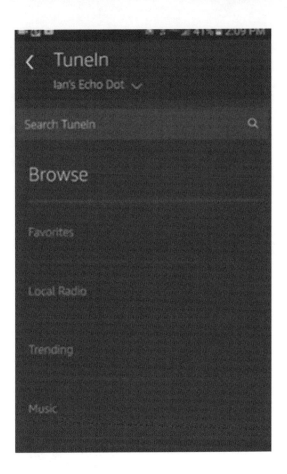

You can then click on favorites on any of the music and play from there.

The best advice I can give you for Tune in is to go on the website using your browser and mark some music favorites so that those favorites are already in there for you. And then once you go to the TuneIn app, you'll see those favorites right there.

How to use voice command to control music

When you want to do this, you should keep your Alexa app open so that it won't find it difficult to connect to the music.

You can say, Alexa, play Radio paradise.

It will respond with, Radio paradise tune in.

You can again say Alexa, play 93.1

You can say, Alexa, play the Rock on station on TuneIn.

Alexa, plays the roots reggae station on TuneIn.

Alexa, play Tom Waits on Pandora.

Alexa, play calm radio blues on TuneIn

Alexa, play the tool station on Pandora.

Without using the Alexa app to find these TuneIn stations and find the names of those Tunein stations, you probably would not be able to voice control those unless if you know the actual station name. So, my suggestion is to add those stations; add whatever stations to your favorites, and then in the Alexa app, you can refer back to your list of favorites and then try to voice command those stations by name.

Pandora seems to respond well to voice commands, say, Alexa, play the Tom Waits station on Pandora, and she says getting your Tom Waits station on Pandora, which is the correct response. What I recommend for the echo dot and controlling music as an overall strategy to get the most out of this music platform is to figure out a couple of stations on Pandora that you like, that you can just easily voice command Alexa to play. Those will be a couple of stations, maybe three or four stations, and then also use TuneIn.

So you want to have a couple of Pandora stations, and you want to have a handful of TuneIn stations, the same number about three or four. The reason is that about half the tune in stations you can control with voice and half of them you can't. So, figure out maybe two stations on TuneIn that you can control with voice that you like and then figure out maybe two stations on TuneIn that don't seem to be able to be controlled by voice that you can just control with the app when you have the time to actually use the app to control the station that plays on the echo dot or the echo.

Chapter Seven

Working with external storage

This chapter will show you how to use external storage to store some of your files. Using external storage has some benefits, and we will talk about just a few of them.

1. External storage can help you speed up your device. When you overuse the memory of your device, it tends to slow it down. This why you need to store some of the excess files you have in the cloud.

2. It can save your life. If you have very important things in your fire 7 and it eventually crashes, all hell will break loose. You will lose your health because

you may not be able to recover those files. But if you have those files on the cloud, you can always get them back.

3. Backup. External storage can be used as a backup for your file. If your device is corrupted with various and you lose some of your files, you don't have to worry because you will always get them back from the cloud.

Manually sync your device.

In this section, you will be learning how to sync your Amazon Kindle Fire manually. Manual syncing is a process that you use to get the information or apps that you have in the cloud onto your Kindle Fire. This should come in handy if you see something that you have already bought on Amazon but don't see it showing up on your Kindle Fire yet. This is very easy to do, but you might not know what that button does if you see on your device. Before you can sync your Amazon Kindle device, you need to be sure you have an active internet connection. Follow these steps to sync your device.

1. Look for the small gear icon in the upper right-hand corner of your device that's your Quick Settings button and click on it.

2. You will then see a quick setting called sync.

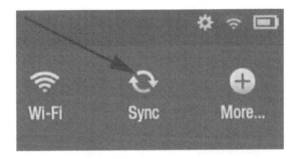

This is the button that will allow you to sync any information, apps, documents, or anything that you have stored in the

Amazon Cloud that isn't quite showing up on your Kindle device.

3. Click on the "sync" icon, and you will see the arrow doing a nice little spin to show you that it's working, and when it's done, you can go back to your home screen and find that content.

Manual syncing is usually reserved for when you have a problem with your Kindle Fire, or you do not see a particular app book or piece of content that you know you purchased that's in the Amazon Cloud, but somehow isn't showing up on your Kindle Fire. You can also use it to manually sync your emails and check for emails immediately as opposed to waiting for your email app to refresh itself.

How to access Dropbox and Google Drive.

Amazon Appstore actually has a Dropbox app, but it's not compatible with the Kindle Fire, so if you search the store, you're not going to find. Another thing is Google Drive. Google Drive also is not available in the Amazon app, so now you can both sideload the Dropbox and Google Drive app. But I want to show you another super-easy way to access all your files without having to do any side loading, and that's using the ES File Explorer app. So, go to the Amazon App Store and install this ES File Explorer app.

On the left side of the app, there are a few menu options one is called Network.

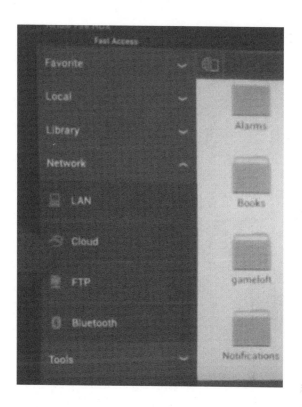

If you pulled out the network, you have land, cloud, FTP, and Bluetooth. Click on cloud, and once you have the cloud opened you have options here to add cloud drives and dropbox.

Click on the "New" button.

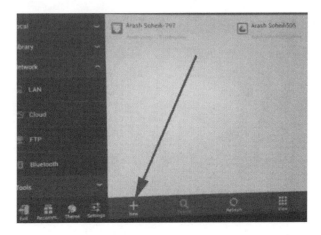

When you click on that button, various applications will show up for you to install on your device.

You can see from the options that there is DropBox and Google drive there.

You can go ahead and install DropBox and Google drive on your device. Once these apps are installed, you would be able to access your entire files store online.

This is a pretty cool way you and use the Google drive and dropbox with your kindle fire 7.

Chapter Eight

How to regain storage space.

I want to show you how to get rid of lower storage if your device is running low on internal storage space. Let's see how much space we have left in this device we want to use for illustration. When you click on setting, and click on storage, you will see how much space is left on your device that has resulted in the notification of low space in your device.

You can see out of 5.6 3gb I only got 112 megabytes in my internal storage and that's what Kindle is complaining about. If you look at my SD card storage I got all of 59.59 GB almost free which is annoying.

So, why are things not moving to the SD card? To see the app that is taking your internal space, click on the "Internal Storage" and you will view all the apps taking much space in your device.

Deleting the apps that you don't use.

To free up space on your device, you have to delete the apps occupying space in your device that you are not using. To do this, click on "settings," "storage," and

"Apps & games." You will then see all the
apps and games installed on your device.

Then look for apps that you think you
don't need anymore and uninstall it.
When you click on any of the games you
want to uninstall, you will see the screen
below.

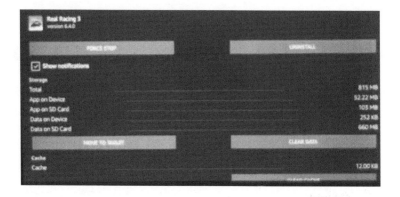

From the screen below, there are four things you can do to the apps, clear the cache, clear data, move to SD card, and uninstall. Let's talk about them one after the other.

1. Uninstall. You can completely remove the install apps from your device by using the uninstall button above. This is to say the apps will completely disappear from your device. If you don't need an app anymore, this is what you need to do to it, completely remove it.

2. Clear Data. When you clear all in data in an app, the app remains installed in your device, but all the data taking place in your device will have been removed. You will see this when you try to clear your data.

Clear Application Data?

This will remove all data for this application including saved content, accounts and settings. The application will remain installed on your device. You should only clear data if the application is seriously misbehaving and you want to have a clean installation of the application.

CANCEL   OK

3. Clear cache. Cache memory is a place where data that your device doesn't use are stored. If you can clear the primary cache memory of any device, it clears up a lot of space in the device. If you see that the cache memory is large, clear it up.

Moving apps to your SD card

When you want to move any app to SD card, the first thing you have to do is to click on the app, and then you will again see this screen.

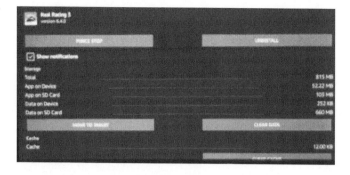

Then click on move to SD card.

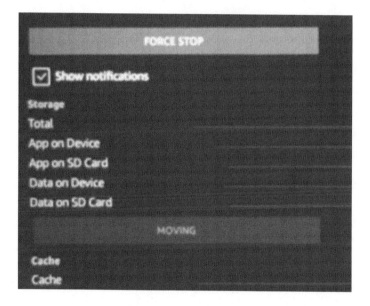

You can see the image above when you click on the apps you want to move to SD card.

Now to check if the app you want to move to SD card is sd card compatible, click on "SD card compatible" to the left of your screen to see all the apps in your device you can move to SD card.

Once you have confirmed that the apps can be moved to the SD card, you can then go ahead and move the app.

Another thing you could do to keep your memory low is to set your device to install any new incoming apps in the SD card. To do this, turn on all the buttons you see in the image below. How to get to that point is, click on "Setting" then click on "Storage" and then scroll down to locate all those buttons.

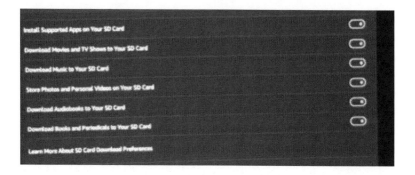

If you do these to your device, you will be able to free up so much space in your internal memory.

Clear the chat history of your social media app.

Another essential thing you need to do to clear up space on your device is to clear the chat history of your social media app. If you use your kindle for your social media communications, the chances are that you have a lot of chat history stored in your device. From experience, I have discovered that WhatsApp alone can take up a lot of space, especially if you belong to many groups. Also, if you chat a lot on WhatsApp, it may have accumulated so much chat history, which has taken a lot of space on your device.

There are two things you can do to solve this problem. You can completely uninstall the social media app and reinstall it, or you clear the chat history only.

Before you think of doing any of the two options, you should have saved any chat that is very important to you because you will lose all your chat history when you do this.

I have already shown you how to uninstall the app. The next thing you need to know is how to clear up chat history in WhatsApp. I will be showing you how to clear up chat history only in WhatsApp. Hopefully, you would be able to do the same with other social media apps.

How to clear up whatsApp chat history.

1. Open up your whatsApp and click on the three dots at the top right of your page.

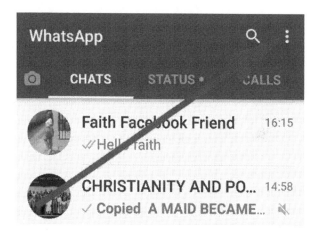

2. Click on "settings"

3. Then click on "chats"

Account
Privacy, security, change number

Chats
Back p, history, wallpaper

Notifications
Message, gr up & call tones

Data and storage usage
Network usage, au o-download

Help
FAQ, contact us, privacy p licy

Invite a friend

4. click on "Chat History"

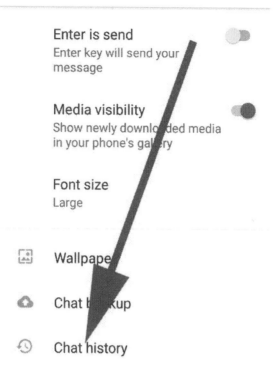

Enter is send
Enter key will send your
message

Media visibility
Show newly downlo ded media
in your phone's gal ry

Font size
Large

Wallpape

Chat   up

Chat history

5. click on "clear all chats"

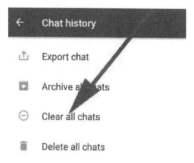

← Chat history

Export chat

Archive a   ats

Clear all chats

Delete all chats

6. The dialog box below will appear.

You can check the two boxes on the dialog box if you want to delete related media and starred massages as you clear the chat history. You can also decide not to check any of the boxes. Once you have decided what to do with the boxes go ahead and click "Clear Messages." Depending on how large your stored chat history is, it will take some time to clear up the chat history.

Clearing up the WhatsApp chat history alone will leave your device with so much space that you will be amazed.

Chapter Nine

How to setup and use Alexa in your device

I'm going to go through the process of setting up the Kindle Fire with Alexa. I am not going to set it up normally, but I'm also going to set it up as if you received this as a gift, and you don't have an Amazon account.

First, turn on the kindle fire. Go ahead and chose your language. And then connect to Wi-Fi. Your device might need to update for a while before it finally comes up, so you have to wait for it.

When you are prompted to put in your number or email for registration, you will need to click on the "New to Amazon" link. Follow the setup process, and your device will guide you on how to go about setting it up from this state.

Once you have finished setting up your device, and you want to ask Alexa any question, you hold down the "Home" button for a few seconds and ask whatever you wish to ask.

That is the "Home" button that the arrow is pointing at there.

How to enable Alexa on your device

If you already have an account with Amazon, and have connected your device to it as shown above, and your Alexa device seems not to be responding, you have to make sure that Alexa is Enable on your device. Follow these steps to enable Alexa on your device.

1. Swipe down your device and click on "settings".

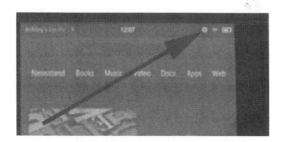

2. Look for "Alexa" and click on it.

3. You have to check if Alexa is enabled. If it is not enabled, then click on the little button to the left to enable it.

Now, you can go ahead and enjoy all the benefits of Alexa in your device.

Chapter Ten

Troubleshooting your device

In this chapter, I will walk you through three things that you can try to fix your Amazon fire your tablet. These steps aren't going to fix every single issue that you might run into, but I'm going to touch on what are some of the most common fixes to problems that you may have. These are going to be resetting your device, making sure you have a good stable internet connection, and then also updating your fire tablet.

What you should do if your table freezes up.

To start off, I first recommend you reset your device. Reset your device by holding down the power button for about 20 seconds, and that's going to completely shut down the fire tablet and take you to a black screen. After that you can go ahead and turn your device back on by clicking the power button, that's going to take you through restart and reboot. Once you open up your fire tablet after that, if you had issues with it being frozen or dealing with some bug, resetting it will probably fix that particular type of problem.

Troubleshooting your wifi connection.

If resetting your device doesn't fix your problem, the next thing I recommend looking at is your internet connection. Swipe down your kindle fire tablet to bring down the quick settings option from the top of the screen.

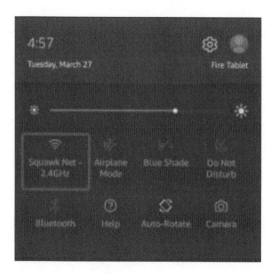

You can see right now I'm connected to my wireless router squawk Net 2.4GHZ. I have a strong signal that I'm getting.

If you're not connected to a wireless router, you will see a Wi-Fi with a slash through it, which means you're not connected to the Internet.

This is when you're going to have a problem in terms of loading different applications that you have to use the internet to access. To tap on that little Wi-Fi setting and it's going to bring up all of the various wireless connections in your area. If you don't see your specific wireless router in the list, you can click on "more settings," and that will bring up all of the different wireless routers that are in your area.

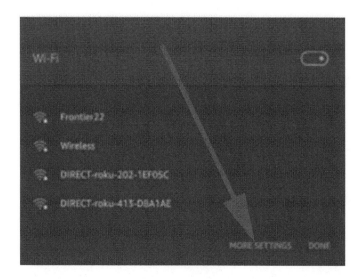

Find your specific wireless router and click on it, make sure you're logged in and connected.

Now, there is a situation where you can be connected to your wireless router, and your internet will still not work. This would be an issue with your wireless router itself. At this point, I recommend you go over to your wireless router unplugging it for about 30 seconds and then plugging it back. It'll go through its restart phase, and hopefully, that will fix your internet issue.

If that doesn't help your internet problem, it could be you have down service in your area. I recommend contacting your internet service provider and ask if the internet is down in your region. They will be able to update you with that information when they hope to get the internet back.

Managing your device update.

If it's not an Internet issue that you're running into, another thing that you could try is updating your device. So, in the quick settings screen on the upper right-hand corner, you see a little gear,

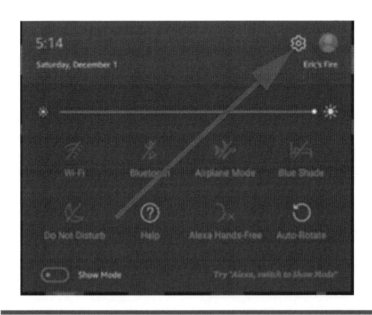

tap on that and then go down to where it says "device options" and then scroll down to "system updates" and click on that, and then right where it says updates click on "Check Now."

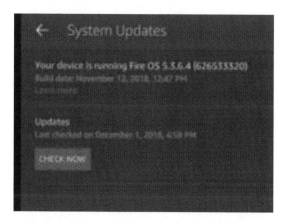

It's going to check to see if there's any critical update that you need to download and install.

So, those are going to be the three different steps that you can try to fix whatever issue you might have run into with your Amazon fire tablet.

Chapter Eleven.

Tips and tricks of the hidden features of kindle fire 7

In this chapter, I will be showing you some cool hidden feature in the kindle fire HD 10 that you can apply to your device and have a more pleasant experience using it.

I want to show you some cool stuff that is going to enhance how you use your tablet by knowing all the cool things that are built. So, let get started by knowing how to change the color of your keyboard.

How to do voice typing with kindle fire 10.

If you are a writer, sometimes you may not want to write with the keyboard as it takes more time than taking to the kindle fire and have it type out what you said. This is one of the coolest features in the device that can help you write much more than you imagine. Think about this. You don't have to sit down to write with your kindle fire 10HD anymore. You can take whatever posture you want and then talk to your device, and it will type out whatever you said. The awesome thing with Google keyboard is that you can directly use punctuation marks while you are talking. For example, if you write to a point where you want to insert full stop, you can say "full stop," and the app will add a full stop to it. You can do the same with comma too.

So, how do you word type with your fire kindle device?

1. Open the word app you want to type into. When you do this, the keyboard should automatically appear. If the keyboard did not appear, click on the word app as if you want to start typing, and the keyboard will appear. Once the keyboard appears, move to the next stage.

2. Click on the mic icon on the keyboard, see the image below.

3. Start saying whatever you want to type out. Whenever you stop talking for some time, the keyboard will return to normal. So, when you want to speak

again, you should click on the mic icon again to notify the keyboard that you want to do voice typing.

How to set the internal keyboard sounds

1. You have to swipe down again and click on "settings."

2. Go back to "keyboard & language."

3. Go to the fire keyboard again.

4. Scroll down to "keyboard sound" and check the box

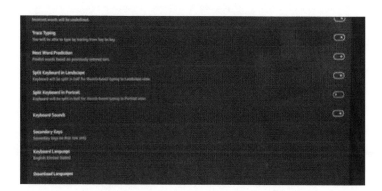

Now, when you use the keyboard you are going to be hearing sounds coming from the keyboard.

How to split the keyboard.

1. Swipe down from the top and click on "Settings."

2. Click on "keyboard & language."

3. click on "fire keyboard."

4. Check these two options, "split keyboard in landscape" and "split keyboard in portraits."

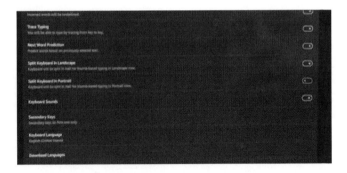

5. You can use the icon on the keyboard to bring the keyboard together to split it. Press and hold done the icon for a few

seconds, and it will split or bring the keyboard together. See the icon below.

How to add special characters to your keyboard.

1. Swipe down from the top and click on "Settings."

2. Click on "keyboard & language."

3. click on "fire keyboard."

4. click on "secondary keys."

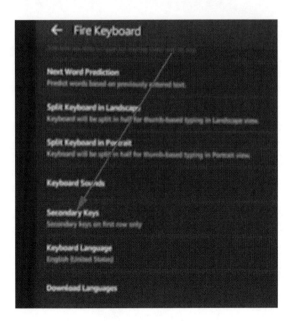

5. Click on "secondary keys on all rows."

This will add the secondary keys to your keyboard. All you have to do is press a key and hold it down for a few seconds to bring out the secondary keys. Then you can pick whichever special character you want to use.

How to multitask with your device.

I will be showing you how you can open more than one app with your device, and all will be left open on your screen. This can be done with an application called multi-screen multitasking. This is a free app that you can download from the play store.

Once you get the app installed on your device, you can run multiple things at the same time. For example, you can open a browser and drag it to the Conner of your device and then open another browser or another program entirely.

This means you could be searching for many things at the same time and all will be open on your screen. Just click on any application you have opened and drag it to where you want it to be on the screen and open another application.

If you are a film lover you an open a film app, and while the film is playing you can search out any information on the web, all at the same time. You have to keep this app open to be able to do all this with your device. In fact, you will have to do all these inside the opened app.

This is how you bring multitasking to the fire tablets which don't have it built-in, but through this app, you can manipulate it. You can also listen to music. If you had musical in your tablet, there's a music option in there that can help you listen to music. Click on the music icon, and it will open up the music control page where you can play, pulse, or stop any music you want to play.

While searching the net, you can also open a note section where you can be typing out notes. Click on the icon you see on the page below to do this.

Set your device to turn off Wi-Fi when you are not using it

The feature we will be using for this is called smart suspend. This how-to get this up.

1. Swipe down and click on "settings."

2. Click on "Power"

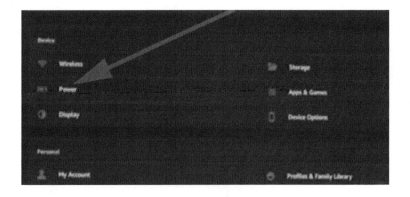

3. Turn on the "Automatic smart suspend"

What this would do is to help you turn off Wi-Fi when you're not using the tablet to help stretch how long the battery lasts because if you're not using the tablet, Wi-Fi doesn't have to be on.

You definitely want to make sure this is checked because that's going to save you a lot of battery. When you're not using the tablet, the battery won't run down so fast. You can also set a schedule and say hey, between the hours of 12:00 midnight and 8:00 a.m., turn off Wi-Fi. Maybe you want Wi-Fi to be on most of the time, but not all the time, you can set the schedule of how you want it to be turned on and off and again all that will help stretch your battery. You should use the next button below the "Automatic smart suspense" to do that.

How to change the background (wallpaper) of the tablet.

1. Again you have to swipe down from the top and go to "settings."

2. Click on "Display"

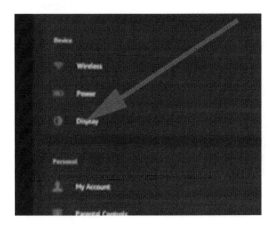

3. Click on wall paper.

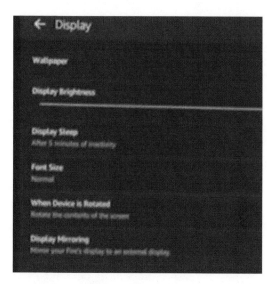

4. You can scroll left and right at the bottom of your screen to pick the wallpaper you like.

5. Finally, click on set to set the wallpaper you have picked as the background of your device.

How to edit your pictures

When you take pictures with your devise, there are so many features that allow you to edit the images you have taken. This is how to open the functions.

1. Take a picture with your device.

2. Open up the picture and click on that little icon the arrow is pointing at.

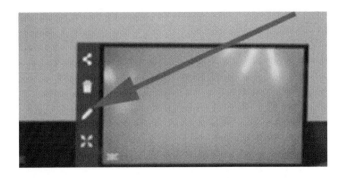

3. You can see a full picture editor function at the bottom of your screen that you can use to edit the pictures you have just taken.

Click on any of the photo editor icons to add any effect you want to add to your picture. Any effect you add that you don't like, don't save it. If you save the effect you don't like, you may not be able to change it anymore. You may need to retake the pictures.

Made in the USA
Las Vegas, NV
07 December 2020

12250344R20088